INFORMA

SHARKS

Christopher Maynard

CANDLEWICK PRESS
CAMBRIDGE, MASSACHUSETTS

ABOUT THIS BOOK

Gripped by sharks? You're about to be! Here's everything you've ever wanted to know about these fearsome fish — and some things you've never even dreamed of!

SECTION 1 ... page 5
Shocking Shark Stories

Sink your teeth into **Splash!** magazine and find out if sharks really are as menacing as they're made out to be. I've put on my journalist's hat to dig out the truth about shark attacks on us, and our attacks on sharks. There's a war on — but who's winning?

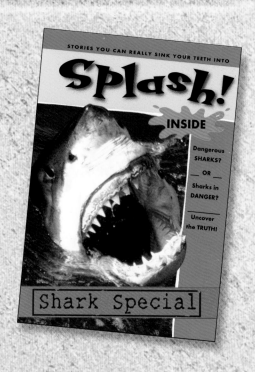

STORIES YOU CAN REALLY SINK YOUR TEETH INTO

Splash!

INSIDE

Dangerous
SHARKS?
— OR —
Sharks in
DANGER?
Uncover
the TRUTH!

Shark Special

Agent Gill
Your mom
called

CONFIDENTIAL

FISH BUREAU OF INVESTIGATION

FBI SHARK FILES

FISH BUREAU OF INVESTIGATION

FILE NO		FILE NO	
75	Shortfin mako	113	Whale shark
76	Bull shark	114	Basking shark
77	Tiger shark	101	Great hammerhead
78	Blue shark	102	Scalloped hammerhead
79	Gray reef shark	103	Cookiecutter shark
80	Sandtiger shark	104	Pygmy shark
99	Thresher shark	105	Tasseled wobbegong
115	Port Jackson shark		Goblin shark
116	Zebra shark		
117	Australian angel shark		
118	Nurse shark		

SECTION 2 ... page 23
Confidential Crime Files

To describe the lethal ways that sharks hunt, I set up the Fish Bureau of Investigation. Then I raided its top secret files for the lowdown on the biggest, the baddest, and the ugliest sharks in the ocean.

If you had to design the deadliest hunting machine in the ocean, your chances of succeeding would be zilch — unless your design was as lean, as mean, and as devastatingly dangerous as the

GREAT WHITE SHARK!

Just what is it that makes sharks so lean, mean, and devastatingly deadly? Exactly how are their bodies adapted to help them hunt and kill? I've collected enough facts on shark anatomy to fill a computer database — so "log on" and get reading!

Not many people know this, but sharks have three different ways of bringing babies into the world! It's all so mind-boggling that I've had to call on the resourceful Miss Skipper and her star pupil, George White, to help me explain it!

G. White

Seaview High

MISS SKIPPER'S BIOLOGY CLASS

SPRING TERM PROJECT

And, finally, to make sure that you've got all the facts at your fingertips, there's a Glossary, a Species List, and of course, an Index.

Christopher Maynard

ABOUT THE AUTHOR

Christopher Maynard has been swimming and diving for years, but has never come face to face with a shark in the wild. He's relieved about this, though he thinks it would be amazing to go on a shark-watching vacation one day. Otherwise, all his shark contacts have taken place in aquariums, seafood restaurants, and at the movies. When not in the water, he spends his time writing books for children. In 1996, he was the winner of the Rhône-Poulenc Junior Prize for Science Books.

ABOUT THE CONSULTANT

During the 40 years that Brian Harris has worked as a professional fish keeper, he has visited aquariums and research centers all over the world, as well as taken part in numerous expeditions to collect sea life, including sharks. He is currently in charge of the aquarium at London Zoo.

STORIES YOU CAN REALLY SINK YOUR TEETH INTO

Splash!

INSIDE

Dangerous
SHARKS?

— OR —

Sharks in
DANGER?

Uncover
the TRUTH!

Shark Special

SHARK BITES

Dear Splash!
I was down at the harbor last week when I saw a tuna fisherman throwing a load of fish scraps over the side of his boat.

As they drifted by, some sharks came up to feed on them. Suddenly, one of the sharks bit at the boat's metal propellers!

What I want to know is this—why on earth would a shark bite something it can't eat?
Puzzled in Adelaide,
AUSTRALIA

Sharks have special sense organs called ampullae of Lorenzini, which let them feel the tiny electrical charges given off by all living things. When metal is placed in saltwater, it creates an electric current that can confuse sharks and make them bite rudders, propellers, and even small boats!

Dear Splash!
Do you know how often great white sharks have to feed?
Nervous in Monterey,
CALIFORNIA

As far as scientists know —and there's a lot they don't yet know about sharks—great whites feed fairly rarely. After a big meal, like a seal, a great white may not need to eat again for a month or more.

Surfboard HORROR!

South Africa ....

Surfer survives hit-and-run attack by great white at popular swimming beach!

A teenager had a narrow brush with death yesterday when he was tossed from his surfboard during a shark attack.

The 17-year-old was just out beyond the breaking waves off Wilderness Beach when a large shark surged up from the water and sank its teeth in the back of his board.

The same bite also tore into the boy's leg, while the ferocity of the blow threw him up into the air and onto the shark's back.

"At first I thought it was a dolphin," said the teenager later, "but I knew I was in real

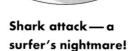

Shark attack — a surfer's nightmare!

trouble when I saw a large fin sticking up."

A lucky escape!
Incredibly, the teenager managed to shove the shark away with his surfboard and then scramble back on the board and ride a wave to the beach.

From the force of the blow, and a tooth fragment found in the board, experts suspect the boy's attacker was a great white shark.

The young man is now recovering in the hospital after a two-hour operation on his leg. Amazingly, he says he'll be surfing again as soon as he's better! ■

The stories on pages 7–10 are based on real events, but the photographs have been changed to protect those involved.

Silent and deadly— a cruising great white.

LIFEGUARDS
to the rescue

Australia ....

Lifeguards battle to free swimmer from jaws of stubborn great white—first in the water, and then on the beach.

Lifeguards at Coledale Beach, south of Sydney, were quick to respond to a swimmer's yells of panic yesterday afternoon as he flailed in chest-deep water a few yards offshore.

At first they thought the 13-year-old boy was drowning. Then they saw the water around him turning pink with blood and realized he was being attacked by a shark.

Six lifeguards dashed to the rescue, but were puzzled when the boy kept shouting even after they reached his side.

Getting a grip

Then, to their horror, they found the shark still had a firm grip on the boy's leg, a grip it refused to let go of.

In the end, both victim and shark (a small great white) were carried back to dry land.

Eventually the shark's jaws were pried from the boy's leg, and he was rushed to the hospital, where he is now recovering after an operation.

The shark has been killed and its jaws preserved — the boy plans to give them to his rescuers, in thanks for saving his life. ∎

Lifeguards are quick to respond to any danger at sea — from drowning to shark attack.

In the last 200 years, 500 shark attacks are reported to have taken place off the Australian coast — fewer than 200 were fatal.

USA ....

Youthful sharks cut their teeth on swimmers' fingers and toes.

Bit-and-run ATTACKS

In a summer of repeated attacks, several unlucky swimmers have had their fingers, elbows, knees, or toes mistaken for supper by hungry young sharks.

Lifeguards reckon a run of stormy weather along the Florida coast has churned up the water. It's left the sea so muddy and murky that the inexperienced young sharks were confused and found it hard to tell the difference between finger-sized fish and fish-sized fingers.

Fortunately, each time the sharks did get a mouthful of human, they realized it wasn't normal food and spat it back out again.

Locals are worried by the unusually high attack rate. But experts say that the increase is due to more people going swimming— in fact, there are a lot fewer sharks around than usual. ■

Hungry young sharks can mistake splashing swimmers for schools of fish.

IN DEEP WATER

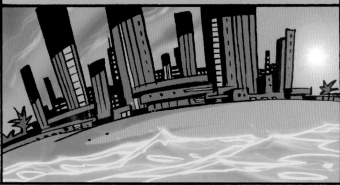

DAWN BREAKS, AND SURF CITY GLEAMS IN THE FIRST RAYS OF SUNLIGHT. THE SCENE LOOKS PEACEFUL ENOUGH, BUT A GRAY REEF SHARK IS CRUISING JUST A FEW HUNDRED YARDS OFFSHORE.

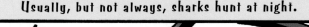

Usually, but not always, sharks hunt at night.

BY LATE MORNING, SURF CITY BEACH IS PACKED WITH PEOPLE.

IT'S ANOTHER PERFECT SUNDAY, FOLKS!

ALERTED BY THE YELLING AND SPLASHING CROWDS, THE GRAY REEF SHARK TURNS TOWARD LAND.

Most shark attacks happen on weekends — when most people go to the beach. More people means more noise, and sound travels a long way underwater.

ALEX BELONGS TO THE LOCAL SWIMMING TEAM. HE'S GOOD, BUT HE STILL NEEDS PRACTICE.

Solo swimmers in deep water run the greatest risk of dying from a shark attack.

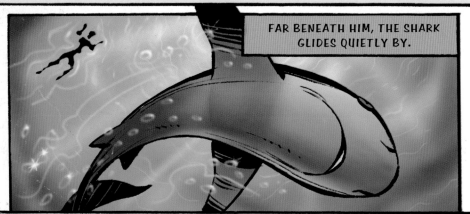

FAR BENEATH HIM, THE SHARK GLIDES QUIETLY BY.

Gray reef sharks mainly eat fish, but they have been known to attack humans.

LIKE ALL HUNTERS, THE GRAY REEF SHARK IS NOSY.

IT SWIMS ON TOWARD THE CROWDED SHALLOWS.

Most attacks take place in waist-deep water — where most people swim and play.

12

ATLANTIC
OCEAN

NORTH
AMERICA

VIRGINIA
1 / **0**

OREGON
1 / **0**

FLORIDA
20 / **1**

CALIFORNIA
1 / **0**

BAHAMAS
1 / **0**

LOUISIANA
1 / **0**

GUADELOUPE
1 / **0**

SOUTH
AMERICA

PACIFIC OCEAN

BRAZIL
4 / **2**

KEY

1 = 1 ATTACK

1 = 1 DEATH

EUROPE

ASIA

AFRICA

INDIAN OCEAN

PACIFIC ISLANDS
1 / 0

AUSTRALIA

MOZAMBIQUE
1 / 1

SOUTH AFRICA
18 / 1

AUSTRALIA
1 / 1

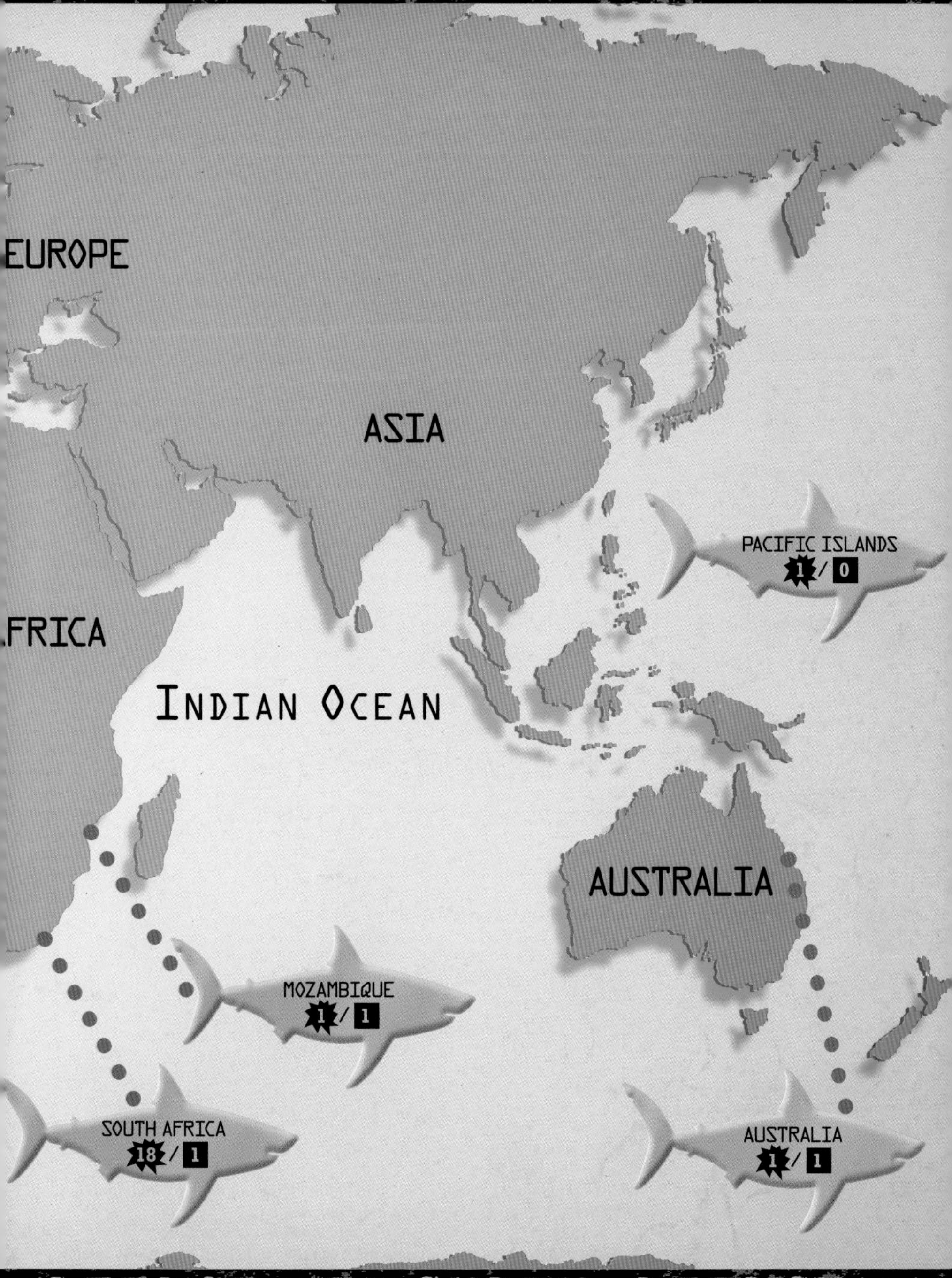

PEOPLE KILLERS — FACE THE FACTS

EACH YEAR, between 30 and 80 people are bitten by sharks. Around 2 to 15 of the victims die as a result. The map on pages 14-15 shows exactly what happened in 1998, for example, when there were more than 50 attacks and 6 people were killed. And that's out of a world population of about 5 billion.

The fact is that death by shark attack is the least of our worries. Each year millions of us are bitten or stung to death by much smaller animals. Malaria-carrying mosquitoes, for example, are responsible for 2 to 3 million deaths annually, while venomous snakes claim 30,000 to 40,000 victims.

The truth of the matter is that sharks are a whole lot better at hogging the news headlines than they are at killing people!

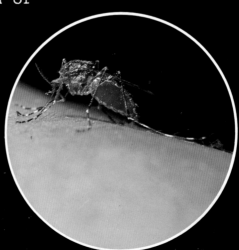

MYSTERY meal means megacatch

Worldwide ....

Not many of us know it, but we eat a lot more shark than we care to admit!

I n Britain it crops up on fish-and-chip menus as "rock salmon." In Australia it's bought as "flake." It's also known as "huss" and "rigg." But these are really all names for dogfish, and dogfish are sharks.

They're the world's most common kind of shark, in fact. But sadly for dogfish, they're also the world's most heavily fished— and not just for the dinner table.

Every last bit

Like all sharks, dogfish are valued for their livers. These are rich in an oil that's used in soaps, perfumes, and skin creams, among other things.

The sharks' flesh is used in cat food, or is mixed with cereals and fed to farm animals. Not even their skeletons are wasted. They're ground up to make fertilizer.

All this adds up to a lot of dogfish. No one knows exactly how many of them are killed every year, but the best guess is an astonishing 75 million pounds! ■

KILLER bites!

USA ....

Death by designer cookery—mighty hunter laid low by health-food fad!

The great white shark, you would think, ought to be able to take care of itself. After all, this shark is the lion of the ocean.

But back in the 1980s, the great white's flesh was found to be lower in cholesterol than almost any other kind of fish.

And since too much cholesterol is thought to increase the risk of a heart attack, the news was enough to turn the mighty hunter into a health-food delicacy overnight.

So much so, in fact, that by the end of the 1980s, millions of pounds of great white shark were being sold.

It turns out that what's healthy for humans is extremely unhealthy for the great white's survival.

But the good news is that people are starting to take notice, and some states have now put a ban on the hunting of this mighty fish. ■

East Asia........

Well over 6 million pounds of fins a year are shipped through Hong Kong alone, to feed the demand for shark fin soup.

In the SOUP

Shark fin soup has long been a delicacy in Hong Kong, China, and a number of other Asian countries.

Even the soup's sky-high price hasn't put a dent in its popularity— it can cost up to $100 a bowl! And with so many people eager to sip it, the search for fins is on.

Follow that fin! The demand is so great that sharks are now being hunted in every part of the ocean.

No size or species is spared, as long as it has thick, good-sized fins.

The fins have become so valuable, in fact, that the shark is often thrown back into the sea finless, leaving it to suffer a slow and extremely painful death.

Millions of sharks are being killed every year to tempt our tastebuds. The sad result is that shark numbers are dropping—at an alarmingly rapid rate. ■

Fins are cut off and dried before being made into soup.

19

Trophy HUNTERS

Worldwide ....

Thousands of sharks are killed for fun, as anglers get hooked on hunting big game.

Each year, thousands of sharks are killed by sports anglers competing to land the biggest specimen, or to catch the most fish within a given period of time.

Their size and fierce reputation make big-game sharks, like makos, a serious challenge to the skills of even the most experienced fisher.

Makos snatch bait with a ferocity that has to be seen to be believed. And once hooked, they put up a mighty battle. It can take four or five hours of bruising struggle to tire them out.

Yet few big-game sharks end up as food.

A proud angler's prize catch— but is it fair game?

Usually, their jaws are removed to make trophies. Everything else is thrown away.

Fortunately, some anglers now mix sport with conservation. After landing a shark, they simply measure it, take out the hook, and return their catch to the water. The anglers have all the thrill of hooking a big one, while the shark lives to fight another day. ∎

DEATH trap

Australia and South Africa ....

Nets protect swimmers from shark attacks, but now sharks need protection from nets!

USE OR ABUSE?

Over the years people have found reasons to prize every part of a shark's body:

🐟 The flesh is eaten (particularly in fish and chips) or dried and ground into cattle fodder.

🐟 The teeth are made into necklaces.

🐟 The skin was once used as sandpaper. Now it's made into leather goods, like shoes and wallets.

🐟 The skeleton is crushed to make fertilizer.

🐟 Liver oil has been used to fuel lamps, lubricate machines, make perfume, face cream, soap.... ■

In South Africa and Australia, lengths of net are often hung from floats a few hundred yards out to sea to guard beaches from shark attacks.

There's a problem, though — the nets don't just stop sharks, they kill them.

Net losses

Well over 1,000 sharks are trapped and die every year in South Africa alone. Other large sea animals are also being taken, including rays, turtles, seals, and dolphins.

Conservationists are so worried that they're looking for ways to reduce the number of deaths. They advise lifting the nets in winter, when fewer people swim, and increasing the mesh size of the nets so they stop only the largest and most dangerous shark species.

That way, smaller sharks would be safe, and only the big ones would be sorry! ■

Shark nets kill 80 percent of the sharks that get tangled in them.

21

END of the line?

Is overfishing pushing sharks toward the brink of extinction?

In the fall of 1996, seven kinds of sharks, including the ferocious great white and the gigantic basking shark, were placed on the World Conservation Union's *Red List of Threatened Species*—a register of animals whose numbers are dwindling fast enough to sound warning bells about possible extinction.

Conservationists reckon that 30 to 70 million sharks are now being caught each year, and that sharks are being killed far more quickly than they can replace their numbers through reproduction.

The problem is that sharks have fewer young than most other fish. And they're slow growers, too—it can be 15 years before some kinds are mature enough to breed.

So when sharks are heavily fished, their numbers take a very long time to recover.

Hook, line, and sinker
Catches are continuing to soar, as fishing fleets meet the ever growing demand for shark meat and liver oil.

But an even greater number of sharks are being killed every year as "bycatch," trapped by accident in nets set for other kinds of fish.

Sharks are among the fiercest predators in the ocean, but their inclusion in the *Red List* is a warning of how easily hunters can themselves be hunted to extinction! ■

Agent Gill
Your mom
called

CONFIDENTIAL

FISH BUREAU OF INVESTIGATION
INVESTIGATION
X 45785

FISH BUREAU OF INVESTIGATION

FBI SHARK FILES

File nos.

File nos.		File nos.	
75	Shortfin mako	133	Whale shark
76	Bull shark	134	Basking shark
77	Tiger shark	198	Great hammerhead
78	Blue shark	199	Scalloped hammerhead
79	Gray reef shark	212	Cookie-cutter shark
98	Sand tiger shark	213	Pygmy shark
99	Thresher shark	214	Tasseled wobbegong
115	Port Jackson shark	215	Goblin shark
16	Zebra shark		
7	Australian angel shark		
	Nurse shark		

FISH BUREAU OF INVESTIGATION

INTERDEPARTMENTAL MEMO

TO: **SPECIAL AGENT GILL**
FROM: **GEORGE C. BASS**

Welcome to the Bureau—good to have you on board. Here are the files you'll need on the main troublemakers—the guys that regularly knock off more fish than anyone else in the ocean.

As you'll see, the folder includes background information (given to all new agents), followed by the files, which have been split into six sections. The first five are grouped by method of attack (deduced from evidence collected at the crime scene). Section six pulls together a few oddballs.

It's all here, from what these guys look like and their average size to the way they operate (their modus operandi). Some of them are hard to get on camera, so where we don't have photographs our people have commissioned an artist's impression based on eyewitness statements.

Best of luck, Gill!

GEORGE C. BASS
Bureau Chief

G.C.B.

Water polo finals— get Bass a poolside seat?

FISH BUREAU OF INVESTIGATION

A Brief Guide for Field Agents

Be warned! There's a vast number of different sharks out there — around 375 species at last count.

They come in all sizes, from a couple of hand-spans long to larger than a bus. But remember, small doesn't mean harmless.

All sharks are meat eaters. Mostly they feed on other kinds of fish, but they'll happily feed on one another, too!

Most sharks have dark backs and pale bellies. It's called countershading, and it makes them a nightmare to spot if you're above them looking down into dark water, or below them peering up into bright sunlight.

Most sharks rest during the day and hunt at night — usually!

If you ever get into a showdown with one, you can count on its pals joining in. Sharks rarely hunt in gangs, but they have a real nose for sniffing out trouble.

Gray reef sharks photographed in a feeding frenzy.

FISH BUREAU OF INVESTIGATION

Know Your Fish

Sharks are fish, of course, but when it comes to identifying suspects, you'll discover that the differences between them and other kinds of fish are more than skin deep.

Start at the head and check the mouth. In most fish it's at the front of the snout, whereas in sharks it's usually underneath. Be careful, though—a few sharks are cunningly disguised as "normal fish," with a mouth at the end of their snout.

To confirm your suspicions, take a look at the throat area. Unlike other fish, sharks don't have gill covers. Instead, they have gill slits, which open straight into the sea. Most sharks have five of them, but a few species have six or even seven.

THIS ISN'T A SHARK

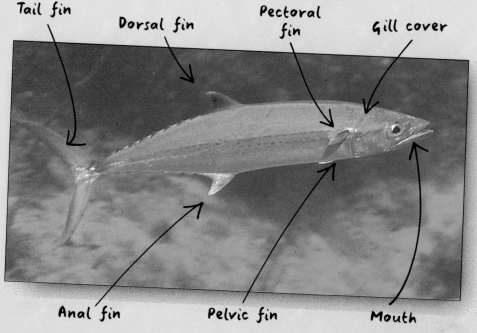

Tail fin · Dorsal fin · Pectoral fin · Gill cover · Anal fin · Pelvic fin · Mouth

THIS IS!

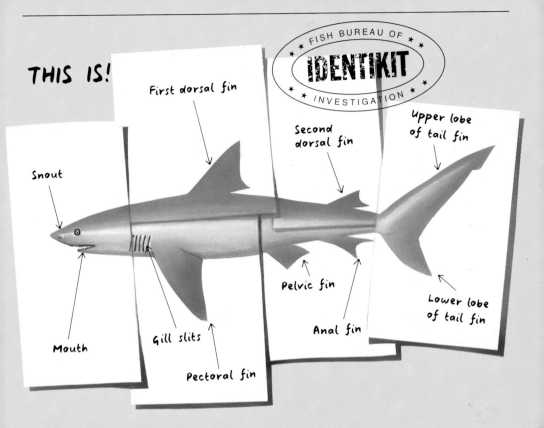

First dorsal fin

Second dorsal fin

Upper lobe of tail fin

FISH BUREAU OF
IDENTIKIT
INVESTIGATION

Snout

Mouth

Gill slits

Pectoral fin

Pelvic fin

Anal fin

Lower lobe of tail fin

Next check the skeleton — but this mustn't be an excuse to injure the suspect! Shark skeletons are made of soft bendy cartilage, whereas in other fish (known as "bony fish") the skeleton is hard stiff bone.

The other main difference is also tough to investigate, but try a gentle squeeze in the stomach region. Bony fish have a gas-filled organ called a swim bladder, which helps them float. Sharks don't. What they do have is a large oil-rich liver. Oil is lighter than water, of course, which is why it helps sharks float when they aren't swimming.

One last tip — always check out a suspect's body shape. Big fast sharks have sleek torpedo-shaped bodies, for example, while a flat steamrollered body shows you that a shark swims slowly and hunts on the seabed.

FISH BUREAU OF INVESTIGATION

Know Your Territory

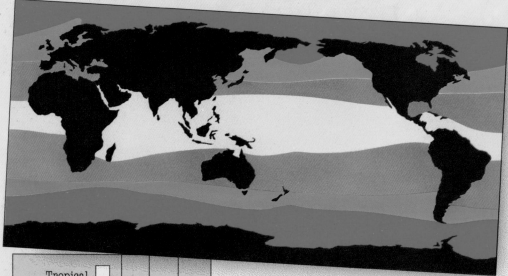

	Tropical	Subtropical	Temperate
Legend			
Tropical ☐			
Subtropical ◼			
Temperate ☐			
Polar ◼			
Australian angel		✔	✔
Basking		✔	✔
Blue	✔	✔	✔
Bull	✔	✔	
Cookie-cutter	✔	✔	✔
Goblin		✔	✔
Gray reef	✔	✔	
Great hammer.	✔	✔	
Nurse	✔	✔	
Port Jackson		✔	✔
Pygmy	✔	✔	✔
Sand tiger	✔	✔	✔
Scalloped hammer.	✔	✔	✔
Shortfin mako	✔	✔	✔
Tass. wobbegong	✔	✔	✔
Thresher	✔	✔	✔
Tiger	✔	✔	
Whale	✔	✔	
Zebra	✔		

The bad news is you'll find sharks in every ocean, and at every level — from surface water (which means from the actual surface down to 600 feet or so) right down to the seabed.

Most shark species hang out near the coast, probably because that's also where most fish are found. But there are a few sharks that like to roam the open ocean.

You'll find different sharks living in different parts of the world. And they're fussy when it comes to water temperature. Most prefer the warmth of temperate, subtropical, and tropical seas.

So play it safe, and plan your next beach holiday at the Poles!

BIG BRUISERS

File nos. 75–79

Here's a posse of smooth operators that are fast and ferocious enough to hunt whatever they want — from slow-swimming turtles to big speedy tuna fish. Most don't mind trying the occasional human, either. Treat them the same way lions and tigers are handled on land. If they're well fed, chances are they won't bother you. If they're hungry, don't even think about stopping to take a photo!

The shortfin mako. Steer well clear of this one!!

Shortfin mako
12 2/3 ft.

Bull
10 1/2 ft.

Blue
10 1/2 ft.

Tiger
16 1/3 ft.

Gray reef
6 1/2 ft.

NAME:
Shortfin mako

TERRITORY:
Surface of open ocean waters; rarely coastal.

DISTINGUISHING FEATURES:
➤ Metallic bluish gray; white underside. ➤ Long slender teeth for stabbing and holding slippery prey.

MODUS OPERANDI:
➤ Probably the fastest shark, capable of 20 mph in short bursts.
➤ Eats bony fish, squid, and octopus, swallowing them whole.

ARTIST'S IMPRESSION

NAME:
Bull shark, alias river whaler

TERRITORY:
Shallow coastal waters and inshore rivers and lakes.

DISTINGUISHING FEATURES:
➤ Charcoal gray; paler underside. ➤ Thick bodied with a short blunt snout. ➤ Broad triangular teeth with jagged edges.

MODUS OPERANDI:
➤ Eats other sharks, bony fish, turtles, birds—almost anything.
➤ A notorious man-eater, largely because it encounters far more humans in rivers and lakes than other sharks do in the open ocean.

FISH BUREAU OF INVESTIGATION

INSTRUCTIONS TO FIELD AGENTS
UPDATE NO. 132/F   SUBJECT: SHARK TEETH

First the good news: Most sharks' teeth are so sharp that you don't feel much pain when they hit you (or so survivors tell us). And now the bad: There aren't all that many survivors. Heed the warning and study tooth shape—it's one of your best clues to how and what sharks eat.

MAKO—long narrow daggers for stabbing and holding prey, which is then swallowed whole.

TIGER—pointed tip for hooking and gripping prey, plus jagged edges for cutting.

BULL—sharp jagged edges for carving chunks out of prey too big to swallow whole.

NURSE—rows of stubby rough teeth for crushing the shells of crabs and lobsters.

NAME:
Tiger shark

- -

TERRITORY:
Surface of coastal waters; often in river estuaries.

- -

DISTINGUISHING FEATURES:
Gray with faint stripes; paler underside. Large head looks almost square because of blunt snout. Big curved teeth with pointed tips and very jagged edges.

MODUS OPERANDI:
Will eat almost anything, from bony fish to birds and sea mammals. Very dangerous to humans.

FISH BUREAU OF INVESTIGATION

LAB REPORT

TO: George C. Bass, Bureau Chief
FROM: I. M. Squeamish, Dept. of Forensics

Just a note to bring you up to date on the tiger shark study. Here's a list of the sort of stuff we keep finding in their stomachs (aside from the usual seafood).

It proves what you thought — they will grab and swallow almost anything they come across!

Chunk of dog	Tin can	Perfume bottle
Plastic bag	Human arm	Plastic bottles
Pumpkin	Tennis shoe	License plate
Small goat	Lumps of coal	Paper cups

NAME:
Blue shark

TERRITORY:
Open ocean waters; surface down to 1,150 feet.

DISTINGUISHING FEATURES:
 Dark violet blue; white underside. Slender body with narrow snout and long tapered pectoral fins. Narrow triangular teeth with jagged edges.

MODUS OPERANDI:
Feeds on small fish, squid, and octopus.

FISH BUREAU OF **APPROVED** INVESTIGATION

NAME:
Gray reef shark

TERRITORY:
Coral reefs, from surface down to 920 feet.

DISTINGUISHING FEATURES:
Dark gray to bronze; paler underside. Has black band along outside edge of tail fin. Teeth triangular; lower ones narrower and less jagged than upper.

MODUS OPERANDI:
Hunts alone, but is found in groups at other times. Feeds on small fish, squid, octopus, lobsters, and crabs. Is aggressive toward humans if disturbed when feeding, but few attacks recorded.

GRABBER GANGS

File nos. 98–99

Sharks mostly hunt alone, but there are exceptions to the rule. Be on your guard for sand tigers and threshers — you can't miss either of them. Sand tigers have a particularly nasty grin, while threshers have an extraordinarily long tail.

Each shark has an unpleasant habit of patrolling in a pack and using the extra numbers to round up schools of small fish and squid. Threshers also use shock tactics. By flailing their tails against the water they create shock waves that stun their victims long enough for them to dart in for the kill.

A sand tiger grins and bares it!

Sand tiger's tooth

Sand tiger 9¾ ft.

Thresher 14⅔ ft.

NAME:
**Sand tiger shark,
alias grey nurse shark
or ragged-tooth shark**

TERRITORY:
Surface of coastal waters.

DISTINGUISHING FEATURES:
Metallic brown to gray, with blotches; paler underside.

MODUS OPERANDI:
Feeds on small sharks, as well as rays, bony fish, squid, crabs, and lobsters. Sometimes hunts in groups.

NAME:
Thresher shark

TERRITORY:
From coast to far out at sea; surface down to 1,215 feet.

DISTINGUISHING FEATURES:
Metallic blue gray; off-white underside. Upper lobe of tail fin as long as the rest of its body. Fairly large eyes. Triangular teeth are short, narrow, and smooth edged.

MODUS OPERANDI:
Powerful swimmer that uses its extremely long tail to herd and then stun its prey. Feeds on small bony fish, such as herring. Only aggressive toward humans if provoked.

LOW LIFE

Sharks that hang around on the seabed are built to suit the places they dine, with a flattened body and skin that's camouflaged to help them hide among rocks and seaweed.

They don't look all that frightening, as they slowly pick their way over the sand. But don't be fooled! These sharks do a professional job of mugging flatfish, like sole and plaice, as well as any lobsters or crabs that wander too near.

By day, Port Jackson sharks huddle together to rest.

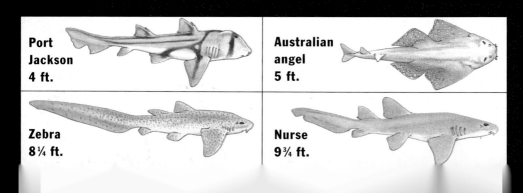

Port Jackson 4 ft.

Australian angel 5 ft.

Zebra 8¼ ft.

Nurse 9¾ ft.

NAME:
Port Jackson shark

TERRITORY:
Seabed of coastal waters, down to 560 feet.

DISTINGUISHING FEATURES:
🐟 Brownish gray, with dark markings; paler below. 🐟 Squarish head, crested above eyes. 🐟 Each dorsal fin supported by a sharp spine. 🐟 Small pointed front teeth; big flat back teeth.

MODUS OPERANDI:
🐟 Slow-moving bottom feeder that hunts at night, returning to particular caves or rock gullies to rest during the day.
🐟 Crunches up sea urchins, crabs, lobsters, and other shellfish.

NAME:
Zebra shark

TERRITORY:
Coastal seabed; common on coral reefs.

DISTINGUISHING FEATURES:
🐟 Yellowish brown to beige, with large dark brown spots; paler underside. 🐟 Very long tail with hardly any lower lobe. 🐟 Has very small teeth, but extremely strong jaws.

MODUS OPERANDI:
🐟 Bottom feeder that eats lobsters, crabs, and other shellfish, as well as octopus and small bony fish, mainly at night.

FISH BUREAU OF
APPROVED
INVESTIGATION

37

NAME:
Australian angel shark

- -

TERRITORY:
Coastal seabed, down to 835 feet.

- -

DISTINGUISHING FEATURES:
- Pale gray to brown, with white spots; paler underside.
- Wide flattened body and head. Long pointed teeth.

MODUS OPERANDI:
- Feeds at night on crabs, shrimp, octopus, and small bony fish.
- Hides, half buried in sand of seabed, to ambush its prey.

FISH BUREAU OF
APPROVED
INVESTIGATION

NAME:
Nurse shark

- -

TERRITORY:
Shallow coastal seabed, down to at least 40 feet.

- -

DISTINGUISHING FEATURES:
- Sandy brown to gray; some have dark spots. Long tail with hardly any lower lobe. Stubby rough crushing teeth.

MODUS OPERANDI:
- Mainly eats bottom-living bony fish, rays, lobsters, and crabs.
- Hunts at night and is very sluggish during the day.
- Known to attack humans only if provoked.

FISH BUREAU OF INVESTIGATION

INSTRUCTIONS TO FIELD AGENTS
UPDATE NO. 194/D   SUBJECT: TAILING SUSPECTS

I know none of you likes to think about it, but swimming for your life is part of the job. The best clue to a shark's speed is the shape of its main swimming tool — its tail.

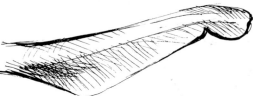

1) Huge upper tail lobe; little or no lower lobe.

1. SLOW MOVERS
These sharks mostly live on the seabed, gliding about with a lazy wavelike body motion.

    Suspects include nurse sharks, zebra sharks, and wobbegong.

2. CRUISERS
Although they aren't particularly fast, these sharks aren't easy to shake off — they can twist and turn like crazy!

    Suspects include bull, blue, and sand tiger sharks.

2) Upper tail lobe much bigger than lower one.

3. RACERS
This tail usually marks a seriously fast swimmer. Don't try to escape — just hide!

    Suspects include makos (probably the fastest sharks) and the great white shark.

3) Upper and lower lobes almost the same size.

BIG SUCKERS

File nos. 133–134

You might think big sharks are more feroci○
Well, you'd be wrong! The world's largest
and the basking sh

A young whale
shark—what
a whopper!

A feeding whale shark (above) and a basking shark (right), their mouths gaping like caves.

GOING WITH THE FLOW

Both sharks feed close to the surface of the water, cruising along at walking speed, their mouths yawning wide to scoop up seawater and food as they go.

It takes hundreds of pounds of tiny seafood to satisfy an adult basking or whale shark. In just one hour, they can take in enough food and seawater to fill a large swimming pool!

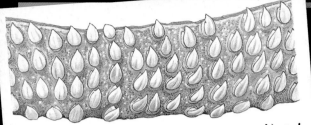

The basking shark's gums are lined with around 3,000 teeth, each one no bigger than a match head.

A basking shark opens wide. Its gill arches are on either side of its throat.

Both the whale shark and the basking shark have teeth, but they're tiny, and nothing is bitten or chewed. Instead, mouthfuls of seawater and food are flushed through gill rakers — walls of spongy mesh hanging inside the gill arches in the throat.

Gill rakers work like tiny fishing nets, trapping and sieving out a slush of seafood, which the shark then swallows whole.

Whale
39⅓ ft.

Basking
29½ ft.

NAME:
Whale shark

TERRITORY:
Coastal and open ocean, in surface waters.

DISTINGUISHING FEATURES:
🐟 Gray to brown, with light spots and checkerboard stripes; white underside. 🐟 The world's largest fish. 🐟 Enormously wide mouth. 🐟 Gums lined with tiny teeth.

MODUS OPERANDI:
🐟 Filter feeder—uses gill rakers to strain out plankton, baby squid, and small bony fish, like anchovies.

★ ★ FISH BUREAU OF ★ ★
APPROVED
★ ★ INVESTIGATION ★ ★

NAME:
Basking shark

TERRITORY:
Surface of coastal waters.

DISTINGUISHING FEATURES:
🐟 Slate gray or grayish brown; paler underside. 🐟 Long narrow "noselike" snout. 🐟 Small eyes. 🐟 Wide mouth. 🐟 Gums lined with tiny teeth. 🐟 Deep gill slits that almost encircle the head.

MODUS OPERANDI:
🐟 Slow-moving filter feeder that mainly eats plankton. 🐟 Sometimes seen feeding in groups of up to 100.

HAMMERHEAD GANG

File nos. 198–199

There's no mistaking these guys. There are nine species, and each one has a variation on the same weird T-shaped head. Their eyes and nostrils are at the ends of the T, by the way. Hammerheads love to eat rays. Even the venomous spine on a stingray's tail can't tear away a hammerhead from its food. After a lifetime of stingray meals, a greedy hammerhead may end up with its throat looking like an old pincushion— completely covered in tail spines.

Hammerheads hunt alone, but may hang out in gangs of more than 100.

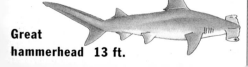

Great hammerhead 13 ft.

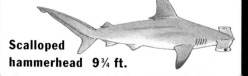

Scalloped hammerhead 9¾ ft.

NAME:
Great hammerhead

TERRITORY:
Coastal waters, down
to 260 feet.

DISTINGUISHING FEATURES:
🐟 Gray brown to bronze; paler underside. 🐟 Largest kind
of hammerhead. 🐟 Smallish jagged-edged teeth; upper ones
triangular, but lower more pointed.

MODUS OPERANDI:
🐟 Feeds mostly on seabed. 🐟 Eats other sharks, rays, bony
fish, crabs, lobsters, octopus, and squid.

★ FISH BUREAU OF ★
APPROVED
★ INVESTIGATION ★

NAME:
**Scalloped
hammerhead**

TERRITORY:
Coastal and open ocean;
surface down to 900 feet.

DISTINGUISHING FEATURES:
🐟 Brownish gray to greenish brown; paler underside.
🐟 Smallish teeth, usually smooth edged; upper ones triangular,
but lower more pointed. 🐟 Scallop-edged "hammer."

MODUS OPERANDI:
🐟 Mainly eats squid and octopus, plus perch, salmon, and other
bony fish. 🐟 Sometimes gathers in very large numbers.

UGLY MUGS

File nos. 212–215

There are a few sharks around that aren't just dangerous— they're downright hideous, too.

Dolphin scarred by a cookie-cutter.

Take the cookie-cutter, for example. It must have one of the most monstrous mouths in the ocean! It's named for the way it clamps its jaws onto its victim, then twists and pulls out a plug of flesh——as neatly as a pastry cutter.

But the all-time prize has to go to the goblin shark. It's the stuff nightmares are made of. Luckily, you're unlikely ever to come across it. Goblins live so deep in the ocean that only a few specimens have ever been found.

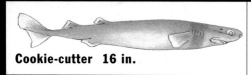

Cookie-cutter 16 in.

Tasseled wobbegong 4¼ ft.

Pygmy 6 in.

Goblin 10⅔ ft.

NAME:
Cookie-cutter shark

TERRITORY:
Open ocean; migrates from surface at night to below 6,500 feet during day.

DISTINGUISHING FEATURES:
🐟 Brown with dark collar around throat.
🐟 Large triangular teeth.

MODUS OPERANDI:
🐟 Gives off a glowing light from its belly to attract prey. 🐟 Takes chunks out of large bony fish or sea mammals; has even scarred the rubber parts of submarines!

NAME:
Pygmy shark

★ ★ FISH BUREAU OF ★ ★
APPROVED
★ INVESTIGATION ★ ★

TERRITORY:
Open ocean; migrates from surface at night to below 5,900 feet during day.

DISTINGUISHING FEATURES:
🐟 Dark brown to black. 🐟 World's smallest shark. 🐟 Narrow upper teeth; bladelike lower ones.

MODUS OPERANDI:
🐟 Gives off a glowing light from its belly to attract prey.
🐟 Eats deep-water squid, and bony fish and crabs near surface.

NAME:
Tasseled wobbegong

TERRITORY:
Coral reefs and coastal seabed, down to 130 feet.

DISTINGUISHING FEATURES:
 Gray brown to yellow brown, with patterned skin and seaweedlike skin flaps on head for camouflage on seabed. Broad flattened body. Sharp daggerlike teeth.

MODUS OPERANDI:
Creeps up on crabs and other shellfish, as well as bottom-living flatfish, such as flounder and sole.

NAME:
Goblin shark

TERRITORY:
Floor of open ocean, to depths of 4,000 feet.

DISTINGUISHING FEATURES:
Pinkish gray; paler underside. Unusually long pointed snout. Beaklike jaws. Soft flabby body. Needlelike front teeth; back teeth flattened for crushing prey.

MODUS OPERANDI:
Very few specimens of this shark have been discovered, so little is known about its feeding habits.

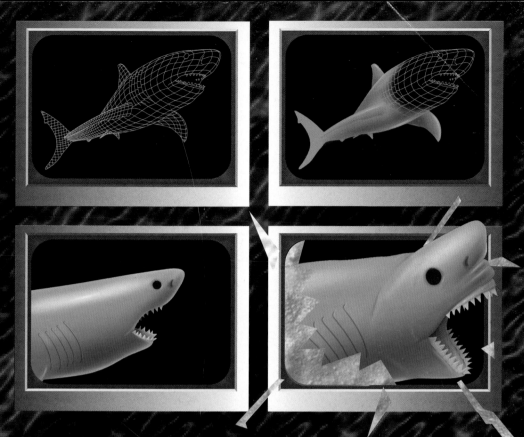

If you had to design the deadliest hunting machine in the ocean, your chances of succeeding would be zilch—unless your design was as lean, as mean, and as devastatingly dangerous as the

GREAT WHITE SHARK!

WELCOME TO THE
INFORMANIA™ database

▲▲▲▲▲

THE PEOPLE-FRIENDLY GUIDE TO
ALL THE INFORMATION IN THE
KNOWN UNIVERSE. PLEASE SCROLL
THROUGH THE LISTING AND HIGHLIGHT
THE TOPIC YOU WISH TO RESEARCH.

SEED
SENEGAL
SENSES
SHAKESPEARE
SHARK
SHEEP
SHELLFISH
SHIP
SHREW

COOKIE-CUTTER
DOGFISH
GOBLIN
GRAY REEF
GREAT WHITE
HAMMERHEAD
LEMON ▶

SHARK PROFILE — THE GREAT WHITE

NAME:
Great white shark,
alias white pointer.

TERRITORY:
Subtropical and temperate
seas; surface of coastal waters.

DISTINGUISHING FEATURES:
❑ Averages 15 feet in length and 1,500 pounds in weight, but can reach 21 feet and 4,400 pounds. ❑ Gray or slate blue in color, with white underside. ❑ Razor-sharp triangular teeth with jagged edges.

BEHAVIOR:
❑ Fast and savage hunter. ❑ Feeds on big fish (including other sharks), as well as turtles and sea mammals, such as dolphins and seals. ❑ Is known to attack humans.

OTHER FILES ARE AVAILABLE. PLEASE SELECT
YOUR NEXT AREA OF INTEREST FROM THE MENU:

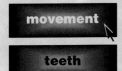 movement   skin   skeleton

teeth   organs   senses

built for speed

Great whites normally cruise along at an easy 1–2 miles per hour. But when they home in on a meal, they torpedo through the water at an amazing 20 miles per hour!

SMOOTH MOVER

So why is the great white such a seriously fast swimming machine? The short answer is that its body is the perfect shape. It's curved and tapered, so water slips smoothly around it without creating the swirling currents that slow things down. This sort of streamlining is

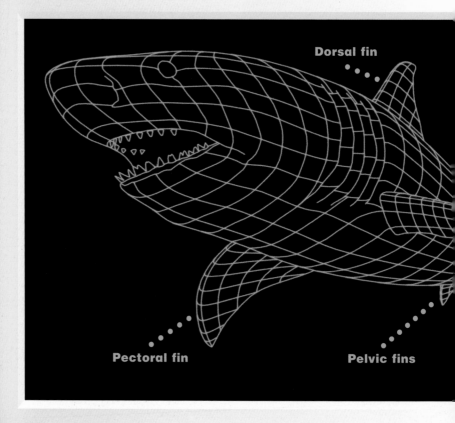

Dorsal fin

Pectoral fin

Pelvic fins

▲ **movement**
● skin
★ skeleton
■ teeth
▼ organs
✦ senses

copied by aircraft and submarine designers searching for every last iota of speed.

ON THE BEAT

Sharks thrust themselves along mainly by beating their tails from side to side against the water. The tail has two parts called lobes, and in the great white and other fast sharks, like makos, these are almost the same size. Evenly sized lobes provide far more speed than uneven ones — in slower shark species, the upper lobe is much bigger than the lower one (to find out more, see page 39).

POWER SUPPLY

So where does all that oomph come from? Muscles, of course. Sharks have big slabs of them all along the sides of their body and tail. In fact, more than half their weight is pure muscle.

Like the other parts of an animal's body, muscles get energy by burning the food and oxygen carried in the blood.

Most sharks are cold-blooded — except, that is, for superfast kinds, like makos and the great white. These sharks are able to keep their blood, and therefore their muscles, warmer than the water they swim in.

And it's because warm muscles produce more power than cold ones that the great white is so fast. This amazing shark's muscles are about twice as powerful as those of cold-blooded sharks.

Upper lobe of tail fin

Pectoral fin

Anal fin

Lower lobe of tail fin

LIFT

Flow of water

WATER WINGS

Like all sharks, the great white glides through water in much the same way that a plane flies through air. The force that keeps it up and stops it from sinking is called lift.

Planes get lift from the way air flows over their wings. Sharks get it from the flow of water over their pectoral fins (the front pair).

What plane wings and shark fins have in common is their airfoil shape — they're more curved above than below. Water and air flow faster over the top of an airfoil than beneath it, and this difference in speed creates lift.

The flow of water over the upper lobe of the tail also gives lift. It tips the shark's head down at the same time, helping the shark's body stay level as it swims.

CONTROLS

Planes use wing flaps and tail rudders to steer. Sharks use their fins. By angling its pectoral fins, a shark can steer in any direction.

Meanwhile, the shark uses its big dorsal fin and smaller pelvic and anal fins to balance its body and stop it from rolling from side to side.

So, put muscles, fins, and streamlining together and what do you get? An undersea version of a jet plane!

▲ movement
● **skin**
★ skeleton
■ teeth
▼ organs
◆ senses

surface conditions

Stroke a shark from nose to tail and it feels silky smooth. Run your fingers the other way and they'll end up scraped or bleeding. How come?

ALL WRAPPED UP

A shark isn't covered in a sheet of hairy skin like a human being. Instead, its skin is an amazing layer of tiny scales called denticles — the word means "small tooth."

The denticles overlap one another like roof tiles. They're as tough as tiles, too, because they're made from the same hard stuff as sharks' teeth. In fact, denticles are so tough

A great white's skin seen through a microscope.

and jagged that if you rub them the wrong way they feel like rough rasping sandpaper.

WITH THE FLOW

Denticles flow back from a shark's nose to its tail, with their tips pointing in the opposite direction of the way a shark travels. Combined with their smooth hardness, this makes shark skin far more streamlined than any artificial material yet invented.

Each shark species has differently shaped denticles. These are a wobbegong's.

flexible framework

Sharks don't have bones—at least, not the same kind that we do. Instead, their skeletons are made of cartilage, the same rubbery stuff that's in our nose and ears.

being limber enough to touch your toes with your nose!

Actually, sharks don't need that strong a skeleton anyway, since although most sharks are fairly large, their bodies are

BENT ON PURSUIT

Unlike the stiff hard bones that make up the skeletons of humans and many other animals, cartilage is light and very bendy. This flexibility comes in handy when you're tracking your prey and you need to make speedy twists and turns to chase and catch it.

Small sharks are a lot more flexible than big ones like the great white. Some can even swing their heads back to their tails if they want to — imagine

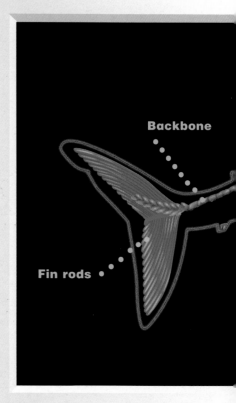

Backbone

Fin rods

▲ movement
● skin
★ **skeleton**
■ teeth
▼ organs
◆ senses

supported by the water they live in. It's the bigger land animals that really need a bony skeleton to carry the weight of their body.

KEY PARTS

The largest single part of a shark's skeleton is the skull, which enfolds and protects key organs, like the brain and eyes.

Just below the skull are the upper and lower jawbones, and behind them are the gill arches.

They support the shark's breathing organs, the gills (to find out more about these, see pages 60–61).

All the fins are stiffened and given shape by thick bundles of cartilage rods. These do the same job as finger and toe bones.

By far the longest part of the skeleton is the backbone. It runs right along the body and into the upper lobe of the tail.

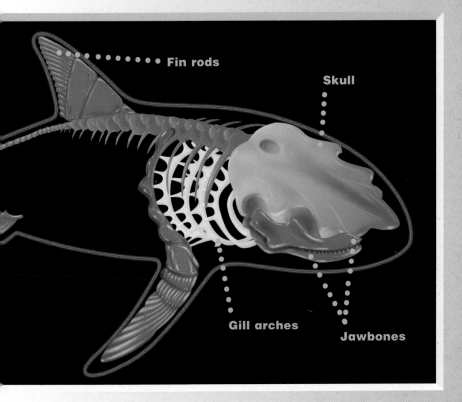

Fin rods

Skull

Gill arches

Jawbones

armed to the teeth

When people scream "Shark!" what they really mean is "Teeth!" It's the cut-and-slash end of a shark that really inspires fear.

WICKED WEAPONS

The great white's teeth are big, sharp, and too plentiful to count. They're weapons to make you break out in a cold sweat.

A 1½-inch-long tooth from the great white's upper jaw.

Different species of sharks have differently shaped teeth — it all depends on what food they hunt (to find out more, see page 31).

Great whites eat anything, from other fish (including sharks) to seals, sea lions, and even the occasional human. Their teeth are jagged, like the blade of a steak knife, and perfectly designed to rip through flesh and bone. And that's not all — the edges are sharp enough to shave hair off your arms!

BACKUP TROOPS

Sharks never run out of weapons. Whenever a front tooth snaps off, a new one swings into the gap. There are more waiting in reserve, too — all folded into the jaw until it's time to move to the frontline.

In young sharks, a complete set of teeth is replaced every two weeks. In adults, one set lasts a month or two. A shark will go through hundreds of sets of teeth in its lifetime — and in the great white's case, a lifetime can be as long as 20 to 30 years.

▲ movement
● skin
★ skeleton
■ **teeth**
▼ organs
◆ senses

JAWS!

In humans, the top jaw is part of the skull. And although the lower jaw is a separate bone, it's hinged to the skull.

Not so in sharks. A shark's skull and upper and lower jaws are completely separate from one another. They're not hinged. Instead, they float free and are linked only by muscles. This unusual arrangement lets sharks do two things that we humans would find impossible.

DOUBLE TROUBLE

First, a shark can open its mouth as wide as its head to swallow huge hunks of food. An adult great white, for example, can gulp down a whole seal!

A great white's jaws can open wider than 3 feet.

Second, it can fling its jaws out in front of its snout — and this means that when a shark strikes its prey, its teeth hit first!

But that's not all. When a large shark like the great white slams its jaws shut, the strength of its bite is awesome. Its muscles can deliver a tip-of-tooth force of some 500 pounds per square inch — which is roughly the same as having three cars balanced on a fingernail.

In fact, its jaw muscles give the great white more than enough power to slice through flesh, bone, or even the supertough shell of a sea turtle!

life-support systems

Tucked inside muscles, skin, and skeleton are the vital organs — the body parts that keep a shark alive and functioning. If they ever break down, a shark will quite simply shut down.

BREATH OF LIFE

Just about every animal needs oxygen — it's used to burn the food carried in the blood and provide the energy needed to stay alive and grow. Land animals breathe oxygen as a gas from the air. Sharks and other fish breathe it as a gas dissolved in water.

To do this, a shark takes seawater into its mouth, then pushes it over breathing organs called gills and back out into the sea through its gill slits. Like most other sharks, the great white has a set of five gill slits on either side of its body.

Many sharks have to keep swimming to make water flow into their mouth and over their gills. But some, particularly bottom feeders, like the nurse shark and the zebra shark, have a clever

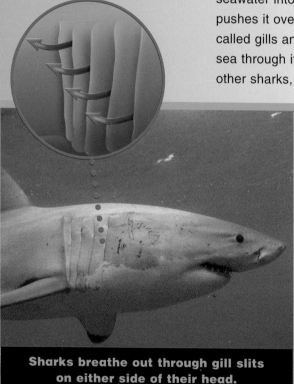

Sharks breathe out through gill slits on either side of their head.

- ▲ movement
- ● skin
- ★ skeleton
- ■ teeth
- ▼ **organs**
- ◆ senses

Gills

Artery

Heart

adaptation. They suck water in through spiracles (a nostril-like hole behind each eye), then pump it down over their gills.

These sharks can lie on the seabed and keep breathing. And since the water comes from above the seabed and not through their mouths, their gills don't get clogged with mud and sand each time they take in a mouthful!

LIQUID ENGINEERING

But how does oxygen get from the water into the shark's blood? Well, inside the gills is a maze of tiny, feathery blood vessels. And the walls of these blood vessels are so thin that oxygen

can pass through them into the shark's blood.

The blood is then pumped by the heart through big blood vessels called arteries to all parts of the shark's body.

REFUELING

Sharks may be meat-eaters and very skillful hunters, but that doesn't mean they need to feed all day and every day. Great whites, for example, are thought to be able to go without food for well over a month without any problems.

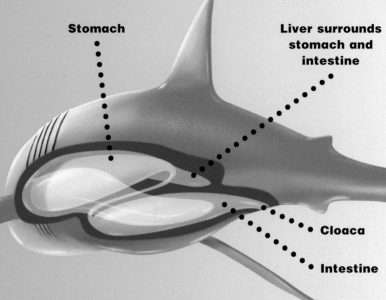

Stomach

Liver surrounds stomach and intestine

Cloaca

Intestine

Sharks don't have to feed all the time because they make the most of what they do eat — their digestive system (the stomach and intestine) is designed to break food down slowly, so every last drop of goodness is squeezed out of it.

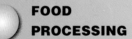

FOOD PROCESSING

Like most other sharks, great whites don't chew their meals — they gulp them down whole. The swallowed slabs of meat end up in the shark's stomach, where a combination of strong chemicals and the churning movement of the stomach walls slowly turns the food into a soupy goo.

From the stomach, the goo gets pushed into a short tube-shaped intestine. This is where food is absorbed into the shark's bloodstream. By now, it's been broken down into such tiny particles that it can pass through the intestine walls.

A shark's intestine has a brilliant design. Inside the tube there's what looks like a spiral staircase. The goo has to travel around and around the spiral, which slows it down and gives the shark's body more chances to take out what it needs.

FILTER SYSTEM

Like humans, sharks have an organ called the liver, which produces chemicals that flow into the intestine, where they help to break down fats. The liver does lots of other things, too, including filtering out anything harmful that may be building up in the blood.

What makes a shark's liver special, though, is its enormous size. It lies in two slabs that surround the stomach and intestine. In a big shark like the great white, it can easily weigh 170 to 200 pounds — as much as a grown man!

END OF THE LINE

A shark's digestive system is so well designed that it takes several days for a meal to pass through the body. Anything that hasn't been absorbed ends up being shoved back into the sea through a body opening called the cloaca.

Sharks also have a neat way of getting rid of fish bones or any other bits of food that their stomach can't digest. They just belch it all out of their mouth!

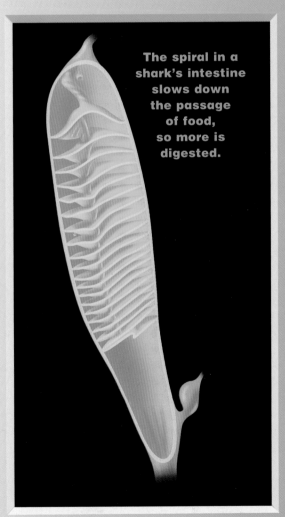

The spiral in a shark's intestine slows down the passage of food, so more is digested.

zeroing in for the kill

So what happens when our lean mean hunting machine starts tracking its prey? That's when all its senses come into play — and a great white on the prowl is almost unbeatable!

SOUNDING THINGS OUT

For a shark, the first clue that some kind of food may be nearby is sound. Scientists don't yet know exactly how well sharks hear, but it's thought they're able to pick up noises from as far as 275 yards away.

No ears flap on the body of a shark, for both are hidden deep inside the skull. All that shows on the outside are two tiny holes on top of the head.

A narrow tube leads from each of these holes to an inner ear, where messages about sound vibrations are sent out along nerves to the brain, the body's control center.

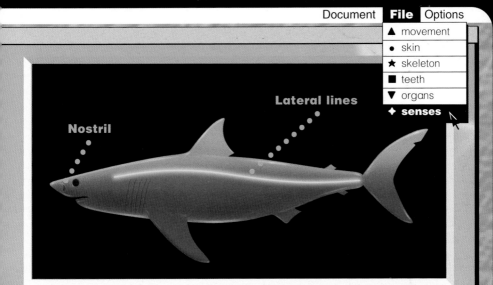

▲ movement
● skin
★ skeleton
■ teeth
▼ organs
✦ **senses**

Nostril

Lateral lines

FOLLOWING ITS NOSE

The great white heads toward the sound. Soon its hypersensitive nose will pick up the trail.

As the shark swims, a steady stream of water flows in and out of its nostrils. Once it catches a whiff of its prey, it turns and faces into the current of water that's carrying the smell.

Then it starts to swim a slow zigzag course. Its head swings from side to side, sampling the water first with one nostril, then the other, so it can figure out where the scent is strongest.

The shark keeps doggedly after the smell, just like a bloodhound, tracking the scent path back to its source.

SUPER TOUCH

A shark's sense of touch is very different from ours. To feel something, we have to be close enough to touch it. A shark doesn't. It can feel things from a long way away.

Sharks can do this because they can sense movement vibrations — the fluttering and quivering that occurs in water when something moves in it.

Movement vibrations are picked up by the shark's lateral lines — a system of tiny tubes that runs under its skin, along the sides of its body. Holes in the skin let the water into the tubes, which are full of hairlike nerve endings that send messages to the brain.

NIGHT SIGHT

The great white is closing in fast now, and its prey is within sight at last.

Like many other big hunters, the great white does most of its feeding at night. Yet even in the dimness of nighttime waters, it has no trouble spotting its victim. Like all sharks, it's able to find its way around at night because its eyes are amazingly well suited to the dark.

At the back of each eye, sharks have a reflecting layer called the tapetum. It acts a bit like a mirror, increasing the light that reaches the nerve endings in the eye. So water conditions that are gloomy to us are clear and bright to a shark.

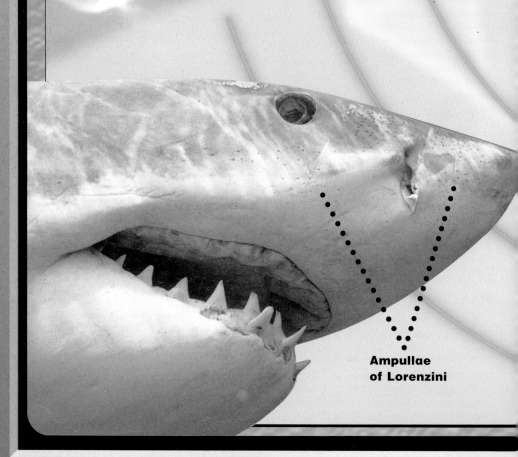

Ampullae of Lorenzini

Electro-sense

Sight

Touch

Smell

Hearing

ELECTRO-SENSE

Seconds before the great white strikes, its electro-sense crackles into action and it locks on to its victim as surely as a guided missile. Now there can be no escape.

The skin of a shark's snout is covered with dozens of tiny pores leading to jelly-filled capsules called the ampullae of Lorenzini.

In water, every living creature gives off prickles of electricity — tiny pulses created by the movement of muscles, like the beating of a heart or the swishing of a tail fin. The ampullae of Lorenzini pick up these incredibly faint signals.

Few other animals have this extra electro-sense. But sharks use it like masters, to end up dead on target!

In the last few seconds before
a kill, the great white's jaws open,
its eyes roll back into its head,
and its snout tips upward.
Its jaws open and push forward
until its teeth and gums stick
out from its mouth.
Then it...

SHUT DOWN YOUR COMPUTER!

G. White

Seaview High

MISS SKIPPER'S BIOLOGY CLASS

SPRING TERM PROJECT

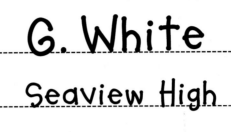

SEAVIEW HIGH

School for the Education of Young Ladies and Gentlemen

BIOLOGY CLASS

For your spring term project, I'd like you all to follow up the work we've been doing in class by writing about how sharks reproduce. Think about the following topics:

* How sharks court and mate.
* How the female's egg is fertilized.
* How the eggs grow into babies.
* How the babies are born.

Don't make up things! Look for useful books in the library, and use their indexes to help you find the information you need.

Don't forget to:

* Underline headings.
* Check your spelling (use a dictionary).

Miss Skipper

Shark Romance

Sharks get romantic only when they want to make babies. Exactly what happens when they mate is mostly a mystery, since even scientists hardly ever see them doing this in the wild.

* Most amusing, George, but you do know that very few sharks eat people, don't you? MISS S.

Maybe sharks eat the scientists who try to study them in the wild! ✳

Scientists mainly study sharks kept in aquariums at zoos and marine parks. Usually, these are the smaller kinds, like dogfish, lemon sharks, and blacktip reef sharks. Small sharks are easier to catch and seem quite happy living in captivity — unlike most bigger sharks, who get sick.

How sharks get together

When people want to go out together, they ask for a date. With sharks, it's different.

The whole thing starts when a female is in the right mood to mate. Nobody knows for sure how often this happens, not even with the sharks that live in aquariums. Probably, it's not very often.

Mmmmm!!

Anyway, the female starts to give off a special scent, which is as big a signal for male sharks as sloshing on a whole bottle of perfume is for people. If a male shark picks up the scent, he stops whatever else he's doing and swims after her. Sometimes whole packs of male sharks will chase a single female.

MISS SKIPPER — I cut out this picture
from a wildlife magazine.

Bites and scars on the body of a female sand tiger shark.

Love hurts

Shark romance is scary. When a male is
interested in a female, he starts nipping her
body and fins. The bites can cut and scar,
which is why some kinds of female sharks have
much thicker skin than the males do. Female
blue sharks have the thickest — it's at least
twice as thick as the males' skin.

Mating

After a while, the female gets fed up and stops trying to swim away. Then they mate.

A male shark's claspers

Male sharks have two body parts called claspers for putting sperm into a female, but they use only one at a time. Claspers are between the pelvic fins.

Aristotle, 384–322 B.C.

ARISTOTLE AND THE CUDDLING SHARKS

The word "clasper" is something we get from Aristotle, one of the most famous scientific thinkers of ancient Greek times.

After observing a pair of claspers up close, he guessed that they were used by male sharks to hold females close during mating.

Aristotle was wrong— which just goes to show that even great thinkers can make mistakes!

MISS SKIPPER — I photocopied this from an encyclopedia.

Females don't have claspers. They use a body opening called the cloaca for mating. It's between their pelvic fins.

Mating doesn't take long, and once it's over the two sharks go their own way. Most likely they never see each other again.

See ya!

Fangs for the memories.

Sharks are weird

Zillions of animals live in the ocean, but hardly any of them mate the way sharks do. With most sea creatures, the female sends a cloud of tiny eggs out into the water, and the male squirts sperm over them. Some eggs bump into a sperm and get fertilized. Others drift away and miss their chance.

Hi!

The amazing thing about sharks is they're just about the only sea creatures that fertilize their eggs inside a female! The only other sea animals that mate in this way are sea snakes and turtles, and mammals like seals and whales.

Some of the sea animals that fertilize their eggs outside their bodies.

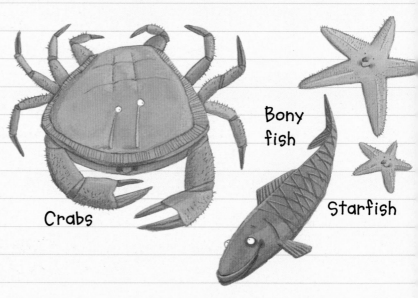

Very fine drawing, George, but starfish don't have faces!

Crabs

Bony fish

Starfish

From eggs to babies

So that's how sharks court each other and mate. What happens next is a bit confusing because the way their eggs develope into babies is different for different kinds of sharks. In fact, there are three ways it can happen.

spelling! develop

76

1) Some female sharks lay their fertilized eggs straight into the sea. The eggs are protected inside egg cases.

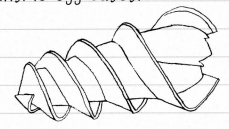

This is my **drawing** of a Port Jackson shark's egg case.

Well done!

2) Most kinds of sharks keep their egg cases inside their bodies. The babies hatch inside the mother and are later born into the sea.

3) A few sharks don't make egg cases at all. The eggs just grow into babies inside the mother's body.

Group 1) # Eggs that hatch in the sea

When a female shark lays her eggs straight into the sea, each one has an egg case and a yolk for the baby shark to feed on. But the eggs are on their own — the mother swims off and leaves them.

Byeee...

These sharks' egg cases are called mermaids' purses, and different kinds of sharks lay slightly different ones. They're not like chickens' eggs, though. *

Sharks that lay egg cases into the sea include:
☆ Most dogfish
☆ Port Jackson sharks
☆ Zebra sharks

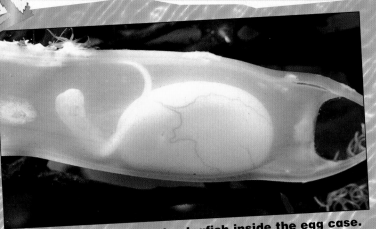

The egg grows into a baby dogfish inside the egg case. It starts off as a tiny pink squiggle attached to a big sac of egg yolk.

MISS SKIPPER— these magazine pictures show a baby lesser spotted dogfish growing inside its egg case.

The baby feeds off the yolk sac as it grows.

When it hatches from its egg case, the baby dogfish is about 4 inches long.

Baby sharks are called pups —just like baby dogs!

Some egg cases lie about on the seabed. Some get snagged on bits of seaweed. Some settle in cracks in the rocks. And if no big fish eats them, they hatch into baby sharks. It's anywhere from 6 to 15 months before they're ready to hatch, depending on what kind of shark they are. When they come out they look just like their parents — only a lot smaller.

Group 2) Egg cases that stay inside the mother

But most sharks do something different. Their eggs grow into babies inside soft egg cases that stay inside the mother's body, in a place called her egg tubes.

There's a yolk sack in each egg case for each baby to feed on. After the babies hatch out of their egg cases, they stay inside the mother while they grow. Then, when they're ready to be born, they come out into the sea through her cloaca.

spelling!

With most of the sharks in this group, it's about 10 months before their babies are ready to be born. But spiny dogfish babies stay inside a very long time — it can be 24 months before they're born!

Sharks that have babies this way include:

☆ Sand tigers
☆ Makos
☆ Threshers
☆ Tiger sharks
☆ Great whites
☆ Angel sharks
☆ Wobbegongs
☆ Spiny dogfish

Group 3) Babies without any egg cases

A few kinds of sharks make eggs that don't have any egg cases at all. The eggs grow into babies in the mother's egg tubes, and each baby is joined to a yolk ~~sack~~. But the babies feed on their yolk ~~sacks~~ only for a short time.

Note spelling!
one sac
two sacs

What happens next is that each baby's yolk ~~sack~~ gets joined to the wall of the mother's egg tubes to make something called the umbilical cord.

Lemon sharks do not produce egg cases.

Sharks that have
babies this way include:

☆ Blacktip reef sharks   ☆ Blue sharks
☆ Gray reef sharks   ☆ Bull sharks
☆ Hammerheads   ☆ Lemon sharks

Each pup comes out tail first and is about 2 feet long.

MISS SKIPPER—lemon shark moms have as many as 12 pups at a time!

Now all the food each baby needs comes straight from its mother's blood, along its umbilical cord. The babies are ready to be born after 8 months to a year.

Umbilical cord

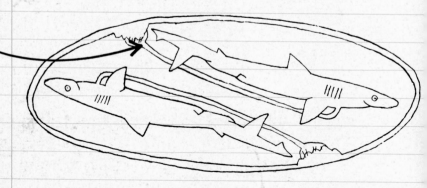

The pup rests for a while, then swims away, tugging at its umbilical cord until it snaps.

Shark families

Most kinds of sharks have between 5 and 15 pups at a time. Sharks never have just one baby, but a few kinds have only two. Tiger sharks are special, though — sometimes they give birth to as many as 60 pups! *

* One record-holding tiger shark had nearly 100 pups!

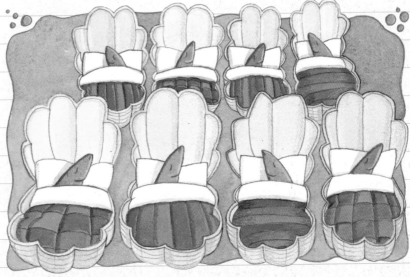

Homeless and alone, too!

After laying their egg cases or giving birth to their babies, mother sharks swim away. The pups are left all alone, with no one to look after them, and lots of them get eaten by bigger fish. It's not fair!

Anyhow, that's why the first thing newborn pups do is shoot off to shallow water, where big fish can't get at them and there are weeds and rocks to hide in. It's only after a few months, when they're bigger, that the pups head for deeper water.

NICE WORK, GEORGE!
I'm impressed by all the facts you've covered and by the improvement in your handwriting. It's a shame about the ink splotches, though—do you need a new pen?

MISS SKIPPER

READY
REFERENCE

GLOSSARY

CAMOUFLAGE

In nature, this is when an animal makes its body blend in with its surroundings. The skin of some bottom-living sharks is patterned and colored, for example, so they can hide on the seabed, either to escape from their enemies or to hunt their prey.

CARTILAGE

The tough rubbery material that shark skeletons are made of; often called "gristle."

The young of most backboned animals develop a skeleton made of cartilage at first, but by the time they're born, almost all the cartilage has been replaced by bone.

CONSERVATION

The protection of the earth's natural resources, ranging from its air, water, and soil to plants and animals.

EXTINCTION

When an animal or plant species dies out, and no more members remain, it is extinct. Dodo birds and dinosaurs are extinct, for example!

FEEDING FRENZY

A kind of mob behavior that sometimes happens when a group of sharks is feeding and there's a lot of food and blood in the water. The sharks seem to go mad, snapping and biting at anything within reach — even one another.

FERTILIZATION

Nearly all baby plants or animals begin with the joining of a male sperm with a female egg. This joining is called fertilization.

FISH

A backboned animal that lives in water and breathes through gills. Scientists have named about 22,000 species of fish. Most fish have skeletons made of bone (and are called bony fish), but the skeletons of sharks and rays are made of cartilage.

GILLS

The organs that fish use to soak up oxygen from the water in which they live. Mammals breathe oxygen from air, and their breathing organs are called lungs.

Fish take water in through their mouths, and push it over their gills and back out into the sea or river again.

The gills of bony fish are protected by a gill cover on the outside of their bodies. Sharks have gill slits that open directly to the sea.

Gill slits

Gill cover

MAMMAL

A backboned animal whose young feed on their mother's milk. There are about 4,000 species of mammals, ranging from humans to cows, giraffes to bats. Sea mammals include dolphins, porpoises, seals, sea lions, and whales.

ORGAN

A body part that does a special job. The heart is the organ that pumps blood around the body, for example, whereas the eyes are organs of sight, and the ears are organs of hearing.

PLANKTON
Tiny plants and animals that float on the surface of seas and lakes. Many kinds can be seen only through a microscope. Animal plankton includes water fleas and small jellyfish species, as well as the eggs and young of larger animals like fish.

PREDATOR
An animal that hunts and kills other animals for food.

PREY
An animal that is hunted and killed for food.

RAYS
A group of fish that have skeletons made of cartilage and are closely related to sharks.

Rays have gill slits, but while a shark's are on the side of its head, a ray's are under its pectoral fins. Most rays have very flattened bodies. Stingrays have spines on their tails.

Stingray

SHELLFISH
A common name for sea animals that don't have a skeleton, and whose bodies are protected by a tough outer shell called an exoskeleton. Besides lobsters and crabs, shellfish include clams, oysters, and mussels.

SNOUT
The tip of a shark's head.

SPECIES
A particular kind of animal or plant. Humans are a species, for example, and there are about 375 species of sharks.

Members of a species share the same body structure and basic features. Usually, reproduction is possible only between two members of the same species.

STREAMLINING
When an object has the kind of smooth curved shape that helps it travel easily through a liquid, such as water, or a gas, such as air.

AS OLD AS TIME

Sharks have been around almost forever. Their ancestors date back to 400 million years ago — that's 100 million years before the first dinosaurs appeared.

BIG TOOTH
The largest shark ever, Megalodon, died out about 12,000 years ago. At 6 in. long, its teeth were almost four times as big as the great white's.

SPECIES LIST

COMMON NAME	SCIENTIFIC NAME
angel shark, Australian	*Squatina australis*
basking shark	*Cetorhinus maximus*
blue shark	*Prionace glauca*
bull shark	*Carcharhinus leucas*
cookie-cutter shark	*Isistius brasiliensis*
dogfish, lesser spotted	*Scyliorhinus canicula*
dogfish, spiny	*Squalus acanthias*
goblin shark	*Mitsukurina owstoni*
great white shark	*Carcharodon carcharias*
hammerhead, great	*Sphyrna mokarran*
hammerhead, scalloped	*Sphyrna lewini*
lemon shark	*Negaprion brevirostris*
mako, shortfin	*Isurus oxyrinchus*
nurse shark	*Ginglymostoma cirratum*
Port Jackson shark	*Heterodontus portusjacksoni*
pygmy shark	*Euprotomicrus bispinatus*
reef shark, blacktip	*Carcharhinus melanopterus*
reef shark, gray	*Carcharhinus amblyrhynchos*
sand tiger shark	*Carcharias taurus*
thresher shark	*Alopias vulpinus*
tiger shark	*Galeocerdo cuvier*
whale shark	*Rhincodon typus*
wobbegong, tasseled	*Eucrossorhinus dasypogon*
zebra shark	*Stegostoma fasciatum*

INDEX

WATER SAFETY

ONLY ONE SHARK EVER SWIMS INTO FRESHWATER RIVERS — THE BULL SHARK.

Pole Position

The Greenland shark is the only shark to live in chilly Arctic waters. It eats fish, seals, and even reindeer.

HARD TO SWALLOW?

The cookie-cutter shark can bite its victims so hard that all its teeth come loose and are swallowed with its food.

FEW TO FEAR

Only 30 or so of the 375 known shark species are thought to be dangerous to humans. All the rest just ignore us!

LONG ODDS

You have a 1 in 300 million chance of being killed by a shark. You're 31 times more likely to die from a bee sting!

Brotherly Love

Sand tiger babies are cannibals. They start off in egg cases in their mother, and the first two to hatch eat all the others!

TROUBLE IN THE AIR

The great white and the tiger shark are the only sharks that can lift their head out of the water.

Pillow Case

Whale sharks are the biggest living sharks and have the largest egg cases. They're about 14 inches long and look a bit like small pillows.

ACKNOWLEDGMENTS

PHOTOGRAPHS

Ardea London Ltd.:
19b; B. & P. Boyle 22; Kev Deacon 5; P. Morris 35t, 48t, 79b, 81; Becca Saunders 36, 37t; Mark Spencer 1; Valerie Taylor 10, 19t, 19m, 25, 45t, 64.

The Bridgeman Art Library:
MAM68929 Marble head of Aristotle (384–322 B.C.) Kunsthistorisches Museum, Vienna 74.

Bruce Coleman Ltd.:
David B. Fleetham 8; Charles & Sandra Hood 41b; Carl Roessler 60; Jeffrey L. Rotmam 40; Kim Taylor 16.

NHPA:
A.N.T. 32, 41t; Norbert Wu 34, 47b.

Oxford Scientific Films:
G.I. Bernard 78, 79t; Tony Crabtree 42; Tui de Roy 45b; David B. Fleetham 8, 33b, 46; Howard Hall 43b; Rudie H. Kuiter 17, 38t; Rick Price 43t; Kim Westerskov 7t.

Planet Earth Pictures Ltd.:
Kurt Amsler 20; Gary Bell 73; Dick Clarke 26; Robert A. Jureit 83; Jon & Alison Moran 58; Doug Perrine 82; Flip Schulke 6bl; Norbert Wu 47t.

Jeremy Stafford-Deitsch:
cover, 30t, 37b, 38b, 44, 57, 66, 68bl.

Tony Stone Images:
Fred Bavendam 21; Simon McComb 7b; Darryl Torckler 29.

Topham Picturepoint: 9.

ILLUSTRATIONS

Rachel Burroughs: 18, 39.
Jonathan Hair: 14–15 (with thanks to Oxford Cartographers).
Emily Hare: 17, 21.
Matthew Lilly: 85, 92.
Katharine McEwen: 69, 71–84.
Philip Nicholson (Thorogood Illustration)**:** 49, 52–57, 59, 61.
Luis Rey: 24, 27, 30, 31, 34t, 35, 48.
Peter Richardson: 11–13.
Michaela Stewart: 86–88.
Ian Thompson: 28, 40–41, 73t.
Peter Visscher: 29, 34b, 36, 42, 44, 46, 48, 62–63, 65, 67.

CREDITS

Edited by **Jackie Gaff**
Designed by **Beth Aves**
Cover design by
Jonathan Hair
Cover photograph by
Jeremy Stafford-Deitsch

With thanks to the **International Shark File** and the **Florida Museum of Natural History** for the statistics on pages 14–16, and to **Keith Lye**.

First U.S. paperback edition 2000

Library of Congress Cataloging-in-Publication Data is available.

Library of Congress Catalog Card Number 97-16537

ISBN (hardcover)
0-7636-0328-7
ISBN (paperback)
0-7636-1043-7

10 9 8 7 6 5 4 3 2 1

Printed in Hong Kong

Candlewick Press
2067 Massachusetts Avenue
Cambridge, MA 02140